THE BOLD

Prayer Warrior

and

Fearless

Intercessor

Prayers that Bring Breakthrough

LaJun M. Cole, Sr. and Valora Shaw Cole

ISBN - 13: 978-1976136641

ISBN - 10:1976136644

Table of Contents

Dedication

This book is dedicated to all prayer warriors and intercessors in every nation of the world that want to go to new levels in prayer and deeper in intercession, with experiencing breakthrough every time.

God is calling for Bold Prayer Warriors and Fearless Intercessors to arise and get into position to watch, guard, and pray against the kingdom of darkness and advance the Kingdom of God.

Welcome

Welcome to **"The Bold Prayer Warrior and Fearless Intercessor Prayer and Study Guide"**. This manual is the advanced version of our first book **"Plug Into The Power of Prayer and Prophetic Intercession"** and was created when God put a mandate on us to go deeper in prayer and intercession. This manual is designed to equip and empower you to pray boldly, intercede fearlessly and to expect breakthrough every time in your life and in the lives of others. You will take a journey in developing a powerful prayer life that reflects your intimacy with God and establishing an effective, strategic intercessor lifestyle through practical teaching, impartation and demonstration. You will experience God and the Holy Spirit in a new way as you gain knowledge, wisdom and understanding from the teaching and impartation of this Prayer and Study Guide.

THE BOLD PRAYER WARRIOR

What is Prayer?

Prayer is the ability to communicate with God that involves both of you speaking and listening. Prayer is a privilege that we have as children of the True and Living God, to come before Him requesting help regarding a particular area of your life or in the lives of others as He attentively listens to your request. Likewise, it is also God's opportunity to speak to us while we listen to Him. It is one of the most powerful tools that is given to the Body of Christ that destroys the works of darkness and manifest the Word of God. We have to be honest with ourselves, walk in humility and cry out to God that we need help and cannot do it without Him. The act of bringing God into every situation and asking Him to change, rearrange, and bring forth the results of our petitions from the supernatural realm into our present according to **Hebrews 11:6.** We must have faith to Believe that He is truly God and He is a rewarder to those that diligently seek Him. Before we pray, it is important for us to repent of any sin that would get us out of alignment with God and hinder our prayers. Prayer is our covenant right as a believer. Praying to get effective results consists of praying the Word of God that relates to your desire and not praying, rehearsing or complaining about the issue or concern. We, as the children of God, through the blood of Jesus Christ, have been given the right to come boldly before God for help (Hebrews 4:16) "Let us therefore come boldly unto the throne of grace, that we may obtain mercy, and find grace to help in time of need."

Personal Prayer Development

As a Christian, we are not just commanded to pray, but to pray always according to **Ephesians 6:18** our lifestyle should be **Praying always with all prayer and supplication in**

3

the Spirit, and watching thereunto with all perseverance and supplication for all saints. For some it is a challenging task because of the lack of knowledge or feelings of inadequacy of how to pray to an Almighty God or even where to begin. Even though we serve the Most High God, He doesn't just want to communicate with us but to also have a relationship that continues to grow. We all start out at one level in prayer but should grow as we build our prayer life that becomes more intimate with our Father.

It is important to establish a strong foundation in prayer and continue to build upon that foundation. Getting desired results consists of praying the Word of God that relates to your desire and not praying, rehearsing or complaining about the issue or concern. We, as the children of God, through the blood of Jesus Christ, have been given the right to come boldly before God for help.

Hebrews 4:16

Let us therefore come boldly unto the throne of grace, that we may obtain mercy, and find grace to help in time of need.

Types of Prayer

The Bible makes reference to nine different types of prayers that we can implement in our life. We will see the principles and concepts of these prayer types by knowing "what" you should pray and "when" you should pray it. An effective prayer life is one of the components to having a strong spiritual foundation. Let's examine the types of prayer found in the Word of God.

1. **Prayer of Praise and Worship**

   This type of prayer focuses centrally and wholly upon God and His characteristics, His majesty, glory, and power, His bountiful beauty and lavish, unconditional love.

   ### I Chronicles 29:10-13

   10 Wherefore David blessed the Lord before all the congregation: and David said, blessed be thou, Lord God of Israel our father, for ever and ever.

11 Thine, O Lord is the greatness, and the power, and the glory, and the victory, and the majesty: for all that is in the heaven and in the earth is thine; thine is the kingdom, O Lord, and thou art exalted as head above all.

12 Both riches and honour come of thee, and thou reignest over all; and in thine hand is power and might; and in thine hand it is to make great, and to give strength unto all.

13 Now therefore, our God, we thank thee, and praise thy glorious name

2. Prayer of Repentance

This kind of personal prayer is asking for the forgiveness of sin from God.

Psalm 51: 1-19

51 Have mercy upon me, O God, according to thy lovingkindness: according unto the multitude of thy tender mercies blot out my transgressions.

2 Wash me thoroughly from mine iniquity, and cleanse me from my sin.

3 For I acknowledge my transgressions: and my sin is ever before me.

4 Against thee, thee only, have I sinned, and done this evil in thy sight: that thou mightest be justified when thou speakest, and be clear when thou judgest.

5 Behold, I was shapen in iniquity; and in sin did my mother conceive me.

6 Behold, thou desirest truth in the inward parts: and in the hidden part thou shalt make me to know wisdom.

7 Purge me with hyssop, and I shall be clean: wash me, and I shall be whiter than snow.

8 Make me to hear joy and gladness; that the bones which thou hast broken may rejoice.

9 Hide thy face from my sins, and blot out all mine iniquities.

10 Create in me a clean heart, O God; and renew a right spirit within me.

11 Cast me not away from thy presence; and take not thy holy spirit from me.

12 Restore unto me the joy of thy salvation; and uphold me with thy free spirit.

13 Then will I teach transgressors thy ways; and sinners shall be converted unto thee.

14 Deliver me from blood- guiltiness, O God, thou God of my salvation: and my tongue shall sing aloud of thy righteousness.

15 O Lord, open thou my lips; and my mouth shall shew forth thy praise.

16 For thou desirest not sacrifice else would I give it: thou delightest not in burnt offering.

17 The sacrifices of God are a broken spirit: a broken and a contrite heart, O God, thou wilt not despise.

18 Do good in thy good pleasure unto Zion: build thou the walls of Jerusalem.

19 Then shalt thou be pleased with the sacrifices of righteousness, with burnt offering and whole burnt offering: then shall they offer bullocks upon thine altar.

3. Prayer of Petition

Petition means to ask for something or make a request. It is asking God for a particular outcome. It is between you and God. We are to be wholly dependent upon God for all of our needs, and He wants us to ask Him for things that we need and desire. This type of prayer is the most used and misused prayer because it will primarily consist of material or personal needs without a kingdom focus. We have to remember to add "Your will be done." God is always concerned about everything that we are concerned about and desires to meet our needs. Yet, it pleases God most when we ask His will through the Holy Spirit. God will answer prayers that line up with His word. It involves faith in God when you pray, not after you pray, not when you feel something, and not when you see something. Several times in Scripture, Jesus says, "according to your faith."

Mark 11:24

24 Therefore I say unto you, what things soever ye desire, when you pray, believe that ye receive them, and ye shall have them.

James 4:3

3 Ye ask, and receive not, because ye ask amiss, that ye may consume it upon your own lusts.

4. Prayer of Thanksgiving

This is a prayer of appreciation for the many blessings and gifts God has given to you. This type of prayer should be part of your everyday life. You are not asking God for something or to do something for you or someone else. When we focus more on what we do have, it isn't as easy to fall into depression because of something that we don't have.

Psalm 118:28,29

28 Thou art my God, and I will praise thee: thou art my God, I will exalt thee.

29 O give thanks unto the LORD; for he is good: for his mercy endureth forever.

5. Prayer of Intercession

This means you are acting in prayer on behalf of someone else, your church, city, nation, etc. in a general or specific way.

Ephesians 1:15-18

15 Wherefore I also, after I heard of your faith in the Lord Jesus, and love unto all the saints,

16 Cease not to give thanks for you, making mention of you in my prayers;

17 That the God of our Lord Jesus Christ, the Father of glory, may give unto you the spirit of wisdom and revelation in the knowledge of him:

18 The eyes of your understanding being enlightened; that ye may know what is the hope of his calling, and what the riches of the glory of his inheritance in the saints.

(Details of intercessor are in the Fearless Intercessor Section)

6. Prayer of Faith

When we pray, we are to believe in the power and goodness of God. It is used to implement God's will for our lives. It is belief that God will change things and conditions as His Word has declared. You are not moved by how things or circumstances appear to be. Instead, you are praying according to what God has said.

James 5:15

15 And the prayer of faith shall save the sick, and the Lord shall raise him up; and if he have committed sins, they shall be forgiven him.

Mark 11:24

24 Therefore I say unto you, what things soever ye desire, when you pray, believe that ye receive them and ye shall have them.

7. Prayer of Agreement (corporate/united prayer)

This type of prayer knits your hearts together through the Holy Spirit. This is where two or more persons come together and agree in prayer for the perfect will of God to manifest in that situation or life. This builds you in love and concern for others.

Acts 1:14

14 These all continued with one accord in prayer and supplication, with the women, and Mary the mother of Jesus, and with his brethren.

Acts 4:31 (23-31)

31 And when they had prayed, the place was shaken where they were assembled together; and they were all filled with the Holy Ghost, and they spake the word of God with boldness.

8. Prayer of Consecration

This type of prayer is done to set ourselves apart to follow the will of God to do what He wants us to do and go where He wants us to go. We are dedicating our lives to used by God as Jesus did.

Matthew 26:39

39 And he went a little farther, and fell on his face, and prayed, saying, O my Father, if it be possible, let this cup pass from me: nevertheless not as I will, but as thou wilt.

Acts 13:2

2 As they ministered unto the Lord, and fasted, the Holy Ghost said, Separate me Barnabas and Saul for the work whereunto I have called them.

9. Prayer of Imprecation

This is used not to bring judgment on the wicked but to come into agreement with God's judgement on them and thereby avenge the righteous. We are instructed in the Word of God to pray for our enemies and love them. Through this appeal, we can see the holiness of God and the certainty of His judgment.

Matthew 5:44-48

44 But I say unto you, Love your enemies, bless them that curse you, do good to them that hate you, and pray for them which despitefully use you, and persecute you;

45 That ye may be the children of your Father which is in heaven: for he maketh his sun to rise on the evil and on the good, and sendeth rain on the just and on the unjust.

46 For if ye love them which love you, what reward have ye? do not even the publicans the same?

47 And if ye salute your brethren only, what do ye more than others? do not even the publicans so?

48 Be ye therefore perfect, even as Your Father which is in heaven is perfect.

Building A Prayer Foundation

The following outline is the foundation to help establish your prayer time and to guide you on how to establish a life of effective prayer based on Luke 11:1-4 where Jesus is teaching His disciples how to pray.

Luke 11:1-4

11 And it came to pass, that, as he was praying in a certain place, when he ceased, one of his disciples said unto him, Lord, teach us to pray, as John also taught his disciples.

2 And he said unto them, When ye pray, say, Our Father which art in heaven, Hallowed be thy name. Thy kingdom come. Thy will be done, as in heaven, so in earth.

3 Give us day by day our daily bread.

4 And forgive us our sins; for we also forgive every one that is indebted to us. And lead us not into temptation; but deliver us from evil.

As we look at this passage of scripture, we can break it down into six distinct areas that will assist in developing a strong foundation for prayer for at least one hour. Each section gives a suggested time to allocate in building your prayer time.

PART ONE (5 Minutes)

Our father, which art in heaven hallowed be thy name thy kingdom come

This Scripture says the disciples asked Jesus to teach them how to pray, and He replied by teaching that they were to begin with the first step with *PRAISE AND WORSHIP*. **Our Father which art in heaven, hallowed be thy name.** Hallowed is the Greek word hagiazo which means to render or acknowledge, to be venerable or hallow. Prayer should start by praising and honoring God. Reference the true and living God as in

I Chronicles 29:10-13 (NIV)

10 David praised the Lord in the presence of the whole assembly, saying, Praise be to you, Lord the God of our father Israel, from everlasting to everlasting.

11 Yours, Lord, is the greatness and the power and the glory and the majesty and the splendor, for everything in heaven and earth is yours. Yours, Lord, is the kingdom; you are exalted as head over all.

12 Wealth and honor come from you; you are the ruler of all things. In your hands are strength and power to exalt and give strength to all.

13 Now, our God, we give you thanks, and praise your glorious name.

In honoring God, it is important to know His names because they reveal His character, who He is, what He does for us and allows us to know the victory that we have in Him. We praise and honor God because He is:

- **El Shaddai** (Lord God Almighty)
- **El Elyon** (The Most High God)
- **Adonai** (Lord, Master)
- **Yahweh** (Lord, Jehovah)
- **Jehovah Nissi (**The Lord My Banner)
- **Jehovah-Raah (**The Lord My Shepherd)
- **Jehovah Rapha** (The Lord That Heals)
- **Jehovah Shammah** (The Lord is there)
- **Jehovah Tsidkenu** (The Lord Our Righteousness)

- **Jehovah Mekoddishkem** (The Lord Who Sanctifies you)

- **El Olam** (The Everlasting God)

- **Elohim** (God)

- **Qanna** (Jealous)

- **Jehovah Jireh** (The Lord Will Provide)

- **Jehovah Shalom** (The Lord Is Peace)

- **Jehovah Sabaoth** (The Lord of Hosts)

PART TWO (25 minutes)

Thy kingdom come. Thy will be done, as is in heaven so in earth

The Word of God is His will! In **Jeremiah 1:12**, the Lord told the prophet Jeremiah that He would hasten (keep watch over) His Word to perform it. We as the Body of Christ have to let our requests be made known unto God.

Philippians 4:6

Be careful for nothing; but in everything by prayer and supplication with thanksgiving let your requests be made known unto God.

It is not that God Almighty does not know our desires or have full knowledge of what we need. When we make known our requests, we acknowledge that we cannot do it within our own strength and are in need of the power of God. When we ask for His will to be done on earth as it is in heaven we are then yielding or submitting our own will for the perfect will of God to be done. When you pray, you have to have an expectation through faith (Pistos (gr.) a firmly relying trust) that you will receive your request.

Hebrews 11:5-7

But without faith it is impossible to please him: for he that cometh to God must believe that he is, and that he is a rewarder of them that diligently seek him"

- Pray for the 5-fold leaders of the gospel that God would fill them with the Spirit of wisdom and revelation in the knowledge of God. Cover them and their families in the blood of Christ from everything that would attempt to exalt itself against the knowledge of God in their lives. **Philippians 1:7-11, Ephesians 3:14-19**

- Pray for your church, the church staff, leaders, and volunteers that God would strengthen them with might and grant them supernatural skill to meet the needs of the people. Pray for ministers in your area to work together in unity and that they would receive revelation knowledge and be rooted and grounded in love and be filled with the fullness of God.

Ephesians 3: 16-19

16 That he would grant you, according to the riches of his glory, to be strengthened with might by his Spirit in the inner man;

17 That Christ may dwell in your hearts by faith; that ye, being rooted and grounded in love,

18 May be able to comprehend with all saints what is the breadth, and length, and depth, and height;

19 And to know the love of Christ, which passeth knowledge, that ye might be filled with all the fullness of God.

- Pray that the Word of God would have free course, be glorified in your church, and that the body of Christ would be delivered from unreasonable and wicked men. **Colossians 2:9-11, 2 Thessalonians 3:1-3**
- Pray for the lost, sick, and oppressed. God's will is that all be saved, healed, and delivered.

2 Peter 3:9

God's not willing that any should perish. In 3 John 2, Paul prays "Beloved, I wish above all things that thou mayest prosper and be in health, even as thy soul prospereth.

- This is a prayer for balance and wholeness.

Proverbs 31:8,9

Open thy mouth for the dumb in the cause of all such as are appointed to destruction" and Open thy mouth, judge righteously, and plead the cause of the poor and needy."

Pray for the abandoned and helpless.

- Call souls into the Kingdom of God. Call out their names and pray for lost loved ones, friends, neighbors, co-workers, and enemies. Break the power of darkness over their minds and hearts

2 Corinthians 4: 4

In whom the god of this world hath blinded the minds of them which believe not, lest the light of the glorious gospel of Christ, who is the image of God, should shine unto them.

Thank God for sending laborers to the harvest of souls.

Matthew 9:38

Pray ye therefore the Lord of the harvest that he will send forth labourers into his harvest.

- Pray for your husband or wife. Speak the Word of God over their lives. Build on their pluses and focus on their strengths… thank God for the good points. Also, call those things that be not as though they were according to **Romans 4:12**. **Wives,** call your husbands the spiritual leaders in the home. Call them full of love, faith, and power. Call them prayer warriors and great men of God. Confess that your husband loves you as Christ loved the church and gave Himself for it. **Husbands,** call your wives loving gentle Proverbs 31 women that have a submissive and quiet spirit.
- Pray for your children. Speak God's Word over them. Bind the enemy that would try to come against your children and speak what God has said about them. Believe and speak **Jeremiah 31:16** over them if they are not living according to God's Word. Confess that you train up your child in the way he should go: and when he is old, he will not depart from it. **Proverbs 22:5-7.**

- Pray for your city, nation, and world. Pray that the latter rain of God's Spirit will fall on your city, nation, and the world. Pray for God's will for your life: holiness, health, and prosperity. Pray for the wisdom of God in your life (**James 1:3**). Pray that you will be led and controlled by the Holy Spirit. Use the power and authority you have been given and release your ministering angels to minister on your behalf. Speak the Word of God over your life.

The Word of God is settled in heaven. Settle it in your heart, believe it in your heart and speak it out of your mouth!

The word of God is vital to our everyday life and continued growth. Several times a day we should get into the habit of praying, confessing, meditating on the word of God and make declarations from His Word , and committing scriptures to memory

1 John 4:4

Greater is He that is in me than he that is in the world.

Romans 8:37

I am more than a conqueror through Jesus Christ.

1 Corinthians 15:57,

But thanks be unto God, Who gives me the victory.

2 Peter 1:4

For by these He has granted to me His precious and magnificent promises, in order that by them I might become a partaker of His divine nature, having escaped the corruption that is in this world through lust.

Ephesians 1:3, I have been blessed with every spiritual blessing.

Colossians 2:10, In Him I have been made complete.

2 Corinthians 5:21, He made Him Who knew no sin to be sin of my behalf, that I might become the righteousness of God in Christ Jesus.

Romans 3:24, I have been justified by His grace through the redemption which is in Christ Jesus.

Revelations 1:6, I have been made a King and a Priest.

Ephesians 2:10, I am complete in Him.

1 Corinthians 2:16, I have the mind of Christ.

Romans 8:11, But if the spirit of Him Who raised Jesus from the dead dwells in me, He who raised Christ from the dead will give to my mortal body.

Acts 1:8, I received power after that the Holy Ghost came up me.

Mark 16:17, And these signs follow me because I believe in the name of Jesus. I cast out devils, I speak with new tongues, I pick up serpents (meaning demons), if I drink any deadly poison if shall not harm me, I lay hands on the sick and they recover.

1 Corinthians 3:21, All things belong to me.

1 Corinthians 1:30, By His doing, I am in Christ Jesus Who became for me wisdom from God, and righteousness, and sanctification and redemption.

Galatians 3:13-14, I have been redeemed from the curse of the law in order that the blessings of Abraham might come upon me.

1 John 3:2, I am the beloved, a child of God.

1 Peter 2:9, But I am a chosen generation, a royal priesthood, a holy nation, His own special people.

1 John 4:17, As He is also am I in this world.

Colossians 1:13, I've been delivered from the power of darkness and transferred in to the kingdom of Jesus Christ.

Galatians 2:20, I have been crucified with Christ, it is not I that lives but Christ lives within me.

Romans 6:8, Therefore we are buried with him by baptism into death: that like as Christ was raised up from the dead by the glory of the Father, even so we also should walk in newness of life.

Romans 6:4, I have been buried with Him through baptism and walk in newness.

Colossians 2:12, I have been buried with Him in baptism, I have been raised with Him through faith in the working of God who raised Him from the dead.

Ephesians 2:5, 6, When I was dead in sin, He made me alive together with Christ, for by grace have I been save, and He raised me up together and made me sit with Him in heavenly places in Christ Jesus – so I have been crucified with Jesus, I have died with Jesus, I was buried with Jesus, I was raised with Jesus and I'm seated with Jesus in heavenly places.

John 17:23, God loves me just as much as He loves Jesus.

Colossians 1:16, I was created through Him and for Him.

Revelations 4:11, For I was made for His pleasure and glory.

Deuteronomy 32:9, God's portion is in me.

Isaiah 38:17, He loved back my life from the pits of destruction.

Jeremiah 9:24, The kindness and compassion of God led me to repent.

Ephesians 1:18, God has made me rich, because I who belong to Christ have been given to Him, I am an inheritance to my Father.

Psalm 23:4, I will fear no evil for my Father is with me and His word and His Spirit they comfort me.

1 Corinthians 12:27, I am the body of Christ and Satan has no power for I overcome evil with good.

Isaiah 54:17, I am far from oppression and fear does not come near me.

Isaiah 54:17, Psalm 1:3, No weapon formed against me shall prosper for my righteousness is of the Lord and whatsoever I do prospers for I'm like a tree planted by the rivers of water.

Galatians 1:4, I am delivered from the evils of this present world for it is the will of God.

Psalm 91:10-11, No evil will befall me nor any plague come near my dwelling for the Lord has given His angels charge over me – they keep me in all my ways and in my pathway is life and there is no death. (Proverbs 12:28)

James 1:22, I am a doer of the Word of God and I am blessed in my deeds...I am happy in those things that I do because I am a doer of the Word of God.

Ephesians 1:18, God has made me rich, because I who belong to Christ have been given to Him, I am an inheritance to my Father.

Psalm 23:4, I will fear no evil for my Father is with me and His Word and His Spirit they comfort me.

1 Corinthians 12:27, I am the body of Christ and Satan has no power for I overcome evil with good.

Isaiah 54:14, I am far from oppression and fear does not come near me.

Isaiah 54:17, Psalm 1:3, No weapon formed against me shall prosper for my righteousness is of the Lord and whatsoever I do prospers for I'm like a tree planted by the rivers of water.

2 Corinthians 8:9, Isaiah 53:5, 6, John 10:10, John 5:24, For poverty He has given me wealth, for sickness He has given me health, for death He has given me eternal life...

Psalm 119:25, It is true to me according to the Word of God.

Psalm 37:4, I delight myself in the Lord and He gives me the desires of my heart.

Luke 6:38, I have given and it is given unto me, good measure, pressed down, shaken together, running over do men give into my bosom.

Philippians 4:19, There is no lack for my God supplies all my needs according to His riches in glory by Christ Jesus.

Romans 5:17, I have received the gift of righteousness and I so reign as a king in life by Christ Jesus.

Psalm 35:27, Abraham's blessings are mine and my Father delights to see me prosper.

John 16:13, James 1:5, The Spirit of Truth abides in me and teaches me all things, He guides me into all truth, therefore I confess I have perfect knowledge of every situation and every circumstance that I come up against for I have the wisdom of God.

Proverbs 3:5, I trust in the Lord with all my heart and I do not lean to my own understanding.

Psalm 138:8, In all my ways I acknowledge Him and He directs my path.

Colossians 3:16, I let the Word of Christ dwell in me richly in all wisdom.

Colossians 1:9, I am filled with the knowledge of the Lord's Will in all wisdom and spiritual understanding.

2 Corinthian 5:17, Ephesians 2:10, 1 Corinthians 2:16, I am a new creature in Christ Jesus, I am His workmanship created in Christ Jesus, therefore I have the mind of Christ and the wisdom of God is flowing within me.

Ephesians 1:17, 18, Romans 12:2, I have received that Spirit of Wisdom and the revelation of the knowledge of Him. The eyes of my understanding have been enlightened, and I am not conformed to this world but I am transformed by the renewing of my mind. My mind is renewed by the Word of God.

Colossians 1:10, 11, I am increasing in the knowledge of God and I am strengthened with all might according to His glorious power.

Philippians 4:13, I can and will do all things through Christ which strengtheneth me.

Ephesians 4:29, I let no corrupt communication proceed out of my mouth, but only a word that is good to edifying that it may minister grace to the hearers. I grieve not the Holy Spirit of God whereby I am sealed until the day of redemption.

Ephesians 4:15, I speak the truth of God's Word in love and I grow up in the Lord Jesus in all things.

Proverbs 4:21-23, I will not let the Word of God depart from before my eyes, for it is life to me, and I have found it to be health and healing to all my flesh.

2 Corinthians 6:16, John 10:10, 2 Peter 1:3, 4, Romans 8:31, God is on my side. God is in me now. Who can be against me? He has given to me all things that pertain to life and Godliness; therefore, I am a partaker of His divine nature.

PART THREE (5 Minutes)

Give us this day our daily bread

Begin to thank God for His supply and pray for the needs of others first. Stand on God's Word and praise Him that all our needs are met.

Philippians 4:19

But my God shall supply all your need according to his riches in glory by Christ Jesus.")

Specifics:

- Pray over the needs of your church and church family that all their needs will be met spiritually, mentally, emotionally, and physically.

- Pray for the homeless and those that are hungry. Pray that their eyes would be opened to the **gospel** and **bind** the spirit of poverty.

PART FOUR

And forgive us our debts as we forgive our debtors

- Search your heart and confess any known sin.

  ### 1 John 1:9

  If we confess our sins, he is faithful and just to forgive us our sins, and to cleanse us from all unrighteousness.

- Ask the Holy Spirit to search your heart and forgive anyone that the Holy Spirit brings to your mind.

  ### Mark 11:25

  And when ye stand praying, forgive, if ye have ought against any: that your Father also which is in heaven may forgive you your trespasses.

- Make a decision to forgive and walk in love with those around you so that you will be forgiven, and your prayers will be answered.
- Examine your life. Do you tithe and give offerings? Are you involved in your church, walking in faith and love.

PART FIVE (5 Minutes)

And lead us not into temptation, but deliver us from evil

- Praise God that you have been delivered from every evil work of Satan (sin, sickness, poverty, etc.).
- Bind the spirits of darkness, rebellion, strife, gossip, witchcraft, sin, and any evil spirit that would attempt to come into your life, church, or city. Loose the spirit of love, faithfulness, peace, unity, faith, prosperity, joy, and praise in Jesus' name.
- Remind the evil one, Satan, that he has been paralyzed

  Colossians 2:15

  15 And having spoiled principalities and powers, he made a shew of them openly, triumphing over them in it"). Know that God has given you dominion over Satan.

  Psalm 8:5, 6

  5 For thou hast made him a little lower than the angels, and hast crowned him with glory and honour. 6 Thou madest him to have dominion over the works of thy hands; thou hast put all things under his feet:"

PART SIX (5 Minutes)

For thine is the kingdom and the power and the glory forever

- **Rejoice** because it is finished, and your prayers have been heard and answered! Remain confident in the power of prayer.

1 John 5:14-15

14 And this is the confidence that we have in him, that, if we ask any thing according to his will, he heareth us:

15 And if we know that he hear us, whatsoever we ask, we know that we have the petitions that we desired of him."

- In Jesus' name. Jesus added his name in:

John 14:13, 14 -

13 And whatsoever ye shall ask in my name; that will I do, that the Father may be glorified in the Son. 14 If ye shall ask any thing in my name, I will do it.

John 15:16

Ye have not chosen me, but I have chosen you, and ordained you, that ye should go and bring forth fruit and that your fruit should remain: that whatsoever ye shall ask of the Father in my name, he may give it you.

John 16:23-26

23 And in that day ye shall ask me nothing. Verily, verily, I say unto you, Whatsoever ye shall ask the Father in my name, he will give it you.

24 Hitherto have ye asked nothing in my name: ask, and ye shall receive, that your joy may be full.

25 These things have I spoken unto you in proverbs: but the time cometh, when I shall no more speak unto you in proverbs, but I shall shew you plainly of the Father.

26 At that day ye shall ask in my name: and I say not unto you, that I will pray the Father for you:

Ephesians 3:20

Now unto him that is able to do exceeding abundantly above all that
we ask or think, according to the power that worketh in us.

End your prayer the way you started – with praise and worship because you know God is faithful to do it.

Matthew 21:22

And all things, whatsoever ye shall ask in prayer, believing, ye shall receive.

Mark 11:24

Therefore, I say unto you, what things soever ye desire, when ye pray, believe that ye receive them, and ye shall have them.

This is a suggested format for your prayer time. Always be sensitive to the Holy Spirit in what to focus on and pray about. He will lead you and guide you.

Intimacy in Prayer:

God is calling each of us to a place of intimacy with Him. He wants a close, affectionate, personal relationship so you will have a deep understanding of Who He is.

We must have an understanding of exactly what God is offering us and what He is requiring in this type of relationship. We have to recognize that we need Him and He desires a personal relationship with us. He wanted us so much that He was willing to sacrifice His Son so that through the Son we can have a close relationship with the Father (John 3:16). He wants to share His heart with us as we reveal our hearts and desires to Him.

We are sometimes hindered in our approach to God because we don't really have an understanding of the loving Father that He is. Intimacy with God only requires for us to passionately pursue Him through relationship.

It is God's desire to supply all of our needs as well as to give us the very desires of our heart. Many times, we pursue things first instead of God because we may think we won't receive what we want or need. Just the opposite is true. If we pursue God first, He will make sure the things that we are desiring with find us. "[9] And I say unto you, Ask, and it shall be given you; seek, and ye shall find; knock, and it shall be opened unto you" (Luke 11:9).

Developing Intimacy with God requires spending time with Him in prayer over a period of time. As you spend time together, you establish trust, your confidence grows, your heart becomes more open and receptive, becoming closer emotionally to each other.

Setting an atmosphere for you to vocalize your love for God and His love for you can be done allocating a certain time and particular place dedicated just for Him whether in your home, car, or another designated place. Playing instrumental worship music will bring a peace to you and sometimes you don't always have to say something to God but as blessed when you are just I His presence.

Posture and Position in Prayer

Our posture is significant in our prayer time. Posture can mean our mindsight or our body positions when we pray. Our mindset is greatly important because it is the how we think in approaching God. When we have the right mindset, we can tap into the supernatural power of God. As we study the scriptures in Acts 2:1 "… they were all gathered on one accord in one place." The disciples along with others were in the right posture or mindset. They were all focused on the same thing at the same time, in expectation of the promise that Jesus told them was coming. According to Alex and Stephen Kendrick[1], The Bible references eight different postures or body positions when in prayer. There is not specific instruction given that requires one to be in a certain body position when in prayer but it can represent honor and adoration to a Most Holy God. We will study these physical positions to see how they can affect our intensity in prayer.

1. **Bowing**

    Bowing is a position one takes when expressing honor and allegiance and is associated with worship. Whether we bow our body or just our head, we are showing out loyalty to God. Moses demonstrated this position when the Lord came down in a cloud around Moses on Mt Sanai, "Moses made haste to bow low toward the earth and worship" (Exodus 34:8). Kind David also bowed, "As for me…I will bow down in reference to You" (Psalm 5:7).

2. **Kneeling**

   The Bible makes reference of dropping to our knees in prayer. During Solomon's prayer at the dedication of the Temple he "knelt down in from of the entire congregation of Israel" (2 Chronicles). Philemon 2:10 lets us know "every knee will bow on heaven and under the earth" before Jesus Christ.

3. **Lying Prostrate**

   There are times that we have to go beyond just bowing or kneeling and position ourselves on our face. We note the priest Ezra read the law to those exiles returned in Jerusalem, "And Ezra blessed the Lord, the great God. And all the people answered, Amen, Amen, with lifting up their hands: and they bowed their heads, and worshipped the Lord with their faces to the ground" (Nehemiah8:6). We see Jesus while in the Garden of Gethsemane before His crucifixion, "And he went a little farther, and fell on his face, and prayed, saying, O my Father, if it be possible, let this cup pass from me: nevertheless not as I will, but as thou wilt" (Matthew 26:39).

4. **Lifted Hands**

   A common expression in prayer is lifting up of the hands. David said, "Let my prayer be set forth before thee as incense; and the lifting up of my hands as the evening sacrifice". The Apostle Paul said, "I want the men in every place to pray, lifting their hands, without wrath and dissension" (1 Timothy 2:8).

5. **Silence**

   Sometimes being still and quiet in prayer can bring great results as we position ourselves before God knowing that He is Who He says that He is (Psalm 46:10). Hannah gives example of her awe and amazement as she was silent before God. She found herself in a desperate place because of her desire for a child, "she was speaking in her heart, only her lips were moving, but her voice was not heard" (1 Samuel 1:13) Not only did God hear her silent prayer but He also answered it.

6. **Lifted Eyes**

   Some may choose to close their eyes while I prayer as a way to limit distractions and to maintain focus. The Bible gives two accounts of Jesus. One when "raise his eyes" before praying at the tomb of Lazarus (John 11:41) and secondly when, "looking up to heaven" as He blessed the five loaves and two fish before multiplying them and feeding the five thousand in the wilderness (Luke 9:16)

7. Lifted Voices

As we lift our hands and eyes in prayer, we can also lift up our voice unto the Lord. David said in prayer, "Give ear to my voice when I call to You My voice rises to God, and He will hear me" (Psalm 77:1).

8. Crying out

David declares "Evening and morning and at noon o will pray, and cry aloud" (Psalm 55:17). There are other instances of praying through crying out including Jesus that "offered up prayers and appeals with loud cries and tears to the One who was able to save Him from death, and He was heard because of His reverence" (Hebrews 5:7).

As stated earlier it is not specified that it is a requirement to be in a certain physical posture while in prayer. Each of these postures can be experienced with a different intensity of the person. You can have a different experience in prayer based on your physical position. Being on your face has a different experience that the person that has their hands lifted.

Seven Steps to Prayer That Bring Results

These steps are valuable to the general structure for effective prayer that brings results.

1. **Prayers that bring results must be based on God's Word.** Power to change your situations and circumstances that you are believing for God to intervene, is inside the His Word. Because the Word of God is God's answer for our lives, we have to start with the answer instead of the problem.

John 15:7

If you abide in me and my words abide in you. Ye shall ask what ye will, and it shall be done unto you.

Notice the beginning condition. Make sure you have God's Word. Have the Word abiding in you and you abide in that Word. What is in you will come out as you pray. You will ask according to the Word of God and here is the guarantee, IT SHALL BE DONE UNTO YOU!

Search the Scriptures and write on paper God's answers from His Word. Take the Word of God and come boldly before Him as His son or daughter and declare it. Read it out loud. **Father, I come boldly before Your throne through the blood of Jesus, and, according to this Scripture or that Scripture where You said this (1 Peter 2:24), I can have what I say because Your Word abide in me and I abide in Your Word.**

It is not as beneficial to write it down on paper and never speak it into the atmosphere. Life and death is in the power of the tongue (**Proverbs 18:21**). God's creative Word must be inside of you and be released out of you.

2. **Begin the application of faith.** Prayer doesn't just stop once you release your prayer. You must now begin the application of faith! You cannot pray one thing and then say other things which totally contradict what you've just prayed. Just as it only takes faith the size of a mustard seed to move mountains, so also it only takes doubt the size of a mustard seed to cancel faith. Hold fast to your confession. Act as though it was already done. To be afraid to confess or to act as though it is not already done is to doubt God's Word. If God spoke it, then He surely will bring it to pass!

3. **Refuse to allow doubt and fear to enter your consciousness.** Be aware of the fact that Satan can work in the areas of suggestions, dreams, and visions. Make sure that you allow none of these things to be part of your thinking. If they do not line up with the Word of God, then you must cast them down by the authority of the name of Jesus according to **2 Corinthians 10:5- "Casting down imaginations, and every high thing that exalteth itself above the knowledge of God, and bringing into captivity every thought to the obedience of Christ."** God has given you authority over your thoughts.

It is possible to have doubt in your head while also having faith in your heart. In order for your spirit to maintain control over your soul (mind, will, and emotions) it is necessary to feed your spirit with the Word of God in abundance. Keeping the Word of God before your eyes, in your ears, and in your mouth in order to write it on your heart. **"If your mouth will put the Word of God in your heart when you don't need it, your heart will put the Word of God in your mouth when you do need it".**

You must make a decision to agree **only** with the Word God has spoken to you, and you will, therefore, have what you say. The promise: **Jeremiah 1:12** - God watches over His Word to perform it. When you add your agreement with the Word God has spoken, you shall have what you ask.

4. **See yourself succeeding and not failing.** To receive anything by faith, it is important that we have an inside visual picture, an inner image of a covenant promise. We don't set our focus on what is seen in the physical world but, instead, on what is promised to us in the Word of God. If you can see it then you can have it.

2 Corinthians 4:18

While we look not at the things which are seen, but at the things which are not seen: for the things, which are seen, are temporal; but the things, which are not seen are eternal.

Make no provision for failure. DO NOT SPEAK FAILURE! ONLY SPEAK SUCCESS! Prepare to receive that which you have prayed.

Romans 13:14

But put ye on the Lord Jesus Christ, and make not provision for the flesh, to fulfill the lusts thereof.

Joshua 1:8

This book of the law shall not depart out of thy mouth; but thou shalt meditate therein day and night, that thou mayest observe to do according to all that is written therein; for then thou shalt make thy way prosperous, and then shalt have good success.

5. **Testify of what you believe.** Don't be afraid to tell it. What you believe is the Word of God. You are not testifying to your experiences but rather to what God's Word says is true. Be mindful that it is God working in you both to will and to do His good pleasure. As your prayers begin to manifest, you must be sure not to boast or give credit to your own ability. Examine your motives. Why do we say what we say? Give God all of the credit and all of the glory. Without God, you can do nothing. There is overcoming power in our testimony. Giving voice to the Word of God by declaring our blood-bought right to what is written.

Revelation 12:11

And they overcame him by the bold of the Lamb and by the Word of their testimony.

6. **Commit to fasting with prayer.** In fasting, we are denying our own selfish will and submitting completely unto God. We fast, sacrificing food, in order to focus upon a hunger for God and His perfect will. Fasting doesn't move or manipulate God. It moves our flesh so we may be able to better discern and hear in the Spirit. *Fasting without prayer equals starvation.* Our desires must die in order to pursue the desire of our Heavenly Father and see it manifested in our lives. Christ gives instructions to see breakthrough in our prayers.

> **Matthew 17:21**
>
> Howbeit this kind goeth not out but by prayer and fasting.

There are fasts of different lengths, and the Bible gives three specific **Types of fasts**: the absolute fast, the normal fast, and the partial fast.

- <u>Absolute fast</u>: You don't take in food or drink, including water.
- <u>Normal fast</u>: You go without food but drink plenty of water or broth.
- <u>Partial fast</u>: Can be interpreted in different ways but should not be included in your sleep time. You may choose to eliminate certain foods or activities such as a Daniel fast.

Seek the Holy Spirit to see what type of fast you should start and for how long He is requiring you to fast. It could be one day, three days, twenty- one days, or forty days. If you feel weak during a fast, use the time to pray and read the Word of God.

7. **Get on the giving end.** If you want results in your life, get on the giving end. When you have a need, God will always ask you to sow some seeds. The way the system works in God's kingdom is that it pays to live a life of giving. Instead of just waiting to see your prayers manifested, by giving, you can determine your measure of return. Giving is as much a spiritual discipline as prayer and fasting.

> **Luke 6:38**
>
> Give, and it shall be given unto you; good measure, pressed down, and shaken together, and running over, shall men give into your bosom. For with the same measure that ye mete withal it shall be measured to you again.

Prayer Watches: Your Time To Pray

The Bible mentions "watches" or specific times of the day or night. There are eight watches within a 24-hour period. Everyone has a prayer watch during the day or night. During these set times, you may have more of an urge to pray or you may be awakened to pray for a specific purpose. We are by God as watchmen to stand watch over our families, leaders, cities, and countries against the enemy's activity and for the manifestation of the plan of God.

When we can watch and be able to see the enemy and announce what He is doing and attempting to do, we can ward off the devil's plans he has to steal, kill, and destroy what God has planned for your lives.

Matthew 24:43

43 But know this, that if the goodman of the house had known in what watch the thief would come, he would have watched, and would not have suffered his house to be broken up.

First Watch (The Evening Watch from 6:00 P.M. – 9:00 P.M.)

- **A time of Quiet Reflection:** This is a time to release anxieties to the Lord before going to sleep, to meditate in order to quiet our emotions, realign our mind, and free our will to do the will of God (**Matthew 14:15-23**). Strongly involve those with an apostolic calling and anointing to break strongholds and walls (**Mark 1:32; Luke 4:40**).

- **Period of Covenant Renewal with God**: Time of asking God to manifest our covenant blessings and decree blessings upon our life, family, church, city, and nation. The evening is the foundation of night and the beginning of the watches. What we do at night determines what happens during the day.

Second Watch (from 9:00 P.M. to 12:00 A.M.)

- During this time, intercessors are able to impact the spiritual realm before the enemy begins to stir trouble (**Psalms 119:62**). During this time, God deals with enemies that are attempting to keep you out of His perfect will.

- Characterized by deep darkness when diabolical assignments and sabotage from the enemy are set in motion. It is important for intercessors to pray for God's protection over their families, cities, and nations (**Psalms 68:1**). Pray aloud **Psalm 59** and **Psalm 68:1-4**.

Third Watch (The Breaking of Day Watch from 12:00 A.M. to 3:00 A.M.)

- **The Witching Hour, time *of great spiritual activity*. *This watch will strengthen your faith.*** It entails the darkest and most demonic activity where witches, warlocks, and Satanists start their incantations. Most demonic activity is during this time because most people are in a deep sleep and not many are up praying to oppose Lucifer. This makes us the most vulnerable (**1 Kings 3:20**).

    Don't allow the fear of witchcraft to move you because God has given you dominion and authority over all things. Pray against satanic attacks on your life, family members, marriages, churches and communities. Declare **Psalms 91:5- 6** which promises divine protection for yourself, family, church, city, and nation.

- **Time to set your day before it begins:** This is a powerful watch to command your morning and set things in order for your day before the devil and his demons have a chance to invade it. "Plane crashes, deaths, job loss, and many other acts of the devil can be stopped during this watch when intercessors obey the voice of the Lord and saturate this time with powerful, Spirit-led prayers" - United in Christ Ministries of Canton.

- **Time to strengthen yourself spiritually and seek direction.** Be vigilant and watch for God's revelation. Experience breakthrough and listen for His plans for your life and territory.

- **Time to pray for release from every prison:**
  - Paul and Silas released from prison (**Acts 18:25**).
  - People of Israel released from Egypt (**Exodus 12:31**).
  - Samson escaped from Gaza (**Judges 16:3-4**)

- **Time to make your case in prayer.**
  Pray for the provision of God to be released and for miracles as we apply the blood of Jesus. (**Luke 11:5-13; Acts 16:3**)

- **Dreams flow during this hour.**
  During this time, God will use dreams and visions to bring instruction and counsel to us as we sleep. God also reveals areas where we need to concentrate our prayers (**Job 33:15**). Before you go to bed, pray against nightmares, the enemy's plots, plans, and devices.

Fourth Watch (The Morning from 3:00 A.M. to 6:00 A.M.)

Is very important because it is the last watch of the night.

- **Time for deliverance, to rise and shine, for resurrection (Exodus 12 and 14).** This is the time Jesus walked on the water to release the disciples from the storm (**Matthew 14:25-33**). This is the time to declare God's will over your life (**Psalms 19:2**).

- **Command your morning!**
  Discipline will cause you to wake up early in the morning and set the atmosphere so the enemy's plans and strategies will fail.

- **Time for Declaring God's Word.**

  This is a time for angelic activity or intervention and a time of blessings from heaven. Angels are released by God go to work on our behalf when we pray. As you declare a thing, it will be established (**Job 22:27-28**).

Fifth Watch (The Early Watch from 6:00 A.M. to 9:00 A.M.)

- **Time that God strengthens Christians (Acts 2:15; Psalm 2:7-9).** Sunrise signifies Jesus Christ, the King of kings and the Lord of lords rises over us (**Malachi 4:2**). Pray for God to heal and restore your body, relationships, family, government and the economy.

- **Time to be equipped by the Holy Spirit for service (2 Corinthians 9:30; Ephesians 4:12).** "Acts 2:15 says it was the third hour of the day" (or 9:00 A.M.) when the Holy Spirit descended in the upper room on the day of Pentecost to equip the 120 disciples for service." As you begin your workday, ask the Holy Spirit to equip you for the day.

Sixth Watch (9:00 A.M. to 12:00 P.M.)

- **Time for a harvest of God's promises.** As a watchmen you should guard and watch for the Word of the Lord to be fulfilled with great expectation concerning the manifestation of God's promises for your life (David in **2 Samuel 7:25-29**)

- **Time for provision to do God's work (Exodus 11: 3-4).** Expect the provision for every God-given vision (**Exodus 12:35-36**) that God wants you to bring forth.

The Seventh Watch (12:00 P.M. to 3:00 P.M.)

- **This is a time of rest and to seek God.**
  - Christ was on the Cross
  - Peter's vision of the clean and unclean animals
  - Daniel went home to pray

- **Time of letting your light shine brighter (Proverbs 4:18)**. This is known as midday or the 6th hour where the sun is at its fullest and brightest. Pray that your light would be bright and not led into any temptation or trap of the enemy.

The Eighth Watch (3:00 P.M. to 6:00 P.M.)

- **Time of Power and Triumphant Glory**. Time of revelation, grace, the voice of the Lord, and triumph.
- **Time to Change or Shape History.**

  God changed history during this watch when Jesus died on the Cross (3:00 P.M.) Through the suffering of Jesus Christ and the shedding of His blood, you have been given power and authority to live triumphant over sin and death. Rejoice!

Hindrances to Prayer

❖ **Doubt**: Hesitancy to believe and unbelief probably the greatest hindrance to unanswered prayer. Having full knowledge of God's perfect and tremendous love, we should never doubt. Instead, we should be as Abraham who staggered not at the promises of God because he knew that God was faithful to perform what He had promised him (**Romans 4:2-21**)

    James 1:6-8

    6 But let him ask in faith, nothing wavering. For he that wavereth is like a wave of the sea driven with the wind and tossed.

    7 For let not that man think that he shall receive any thing of the Lord.

    8 A double minded man is unstable in all his ways.

❖ **Self: God hates pride!** Pride prevents sincere prayer because it prevents humility. Prayer is not the time to criticize others. Self must be dethroned. When our aim is to glorify God, He is willing to answer our prayers.

    1 Corinthians 4:7

    7 For who maketh thee to differ from another? and what hast thou that thou didst not receive? now if thou didst receive it, why dost thou glory, as if thou hadst not received it?

❖ **Unlove:** (possibly one of the greatest hindrances). God is love and demonstrates it unconditionally. We cannot be wrong with man and right with God. Neither can we dislike whom God loves.

1 John 4:20

^{20} If a man say, I love God, and hateth his brother, he is a liar: for he that loveth not his brother whom he hath seen, how can he love God whom he hath not seen?

Matthew 5:44-45

$^{44.}$ But I say unto you, Love your enemies, bless them that curse you, do good to them that hate you, and pray for them which despitefully use you, and persecute you; ^{45} That ye may be the children of your Father which is in heaven: for he maketh his sun to rise on the evil and on the good, and sendeth rain on the just and on the unjust. We are to pray for those that persecute us in order to be the sons of God.

❖ **Refusal to do your part.** Love calls forth compassion and service at the sight of sin and suffering. We have to use our gifts, our prayers, and our service. We cannot be sincere in praying for the conversion of the ungodly unless we are willing to make some attempt to bring them under the influence of the gospel. You don't have to pray and ask God for something you already have the ability to do.

Acts 17:16

^{16} Now while Paul waited for them at Athens, his spirit was stirred in him, when he saw the city wholly given to idolatry.

❖ **Praying only in secret may be a hindrance.** God honors united, corporate and "agreed" prayer with others. We were never designed to do everything alone, including prayer.

Matthew 18:19-20

19 Again I say unto you, That if two of you shall agree on earth as touching anything that they shall ask, it shall be done for them of my Father which is in heaven.

20 For where two or three are gathered together in my name, there am I in the midst of them.

❖ **Unforgiveness.** Unforgiveness causes you to hurt yourself. You cannot enter prayer with bitterness and expect to come out with blessings if you don't walk in forgiveness.

Matthew 6:14-15

14 For if ye forgive men their trespasses, your heavenly Father will also forgive you:

15 But if ye forgive not men their trespasses, neither will your Father forgive your trespasses. Forgiveness allows your heart to be made right before the Lord.

❖ **Wrong motives:** When our motives are not right, our prayer does not have power. Your prayers shouldn't benefit you alone but should also help the kingdom of God.

James 4:3

3 Ye ask, and receive not, because ye ask amiss, that ye may consume *it* upon your lusts.

❖ **Idols in our life:** As you look into your life regarding your career, possessions, and family, are you willing to give them up for God? If you are not, they have become idols. When we remove idols, we become ripe for God to bring revival in our lives.

Ezekiel 14:3

3 Son of man, these men have set up their idols in their heart, and put the stumbling block of their iniquity before their face: should I be inquired of at all by them?

❖ **Disregard for God's Sovereignty:** It is important that we follow the example Christ gave to the disciples to begin prayer by honoring God for who He is as the only one who is sovereign and in charge. We, therefore, must understand the divine authority we have been given as lawful heirs, children under His authority.

Matthew 6:9-10

9 After this manner therefore pray ye: Our Father which art in heaven, Hallowed be thy name.

10 Thy kingdom come; Thy will be done in earth, as it is in heaven.

❖ **Unsurrendered will:** God promises to answer the prayers and grant the requests of those who are surrendered to Him. This shows that we have a relationship with God and that we are dependent upon Him as described in the parable of the vine and the branches for life, power, and the ability to produce. We have to know that He knows what is best for us and accept that.

Matthew 6:10

10 Thy kingdom come, Thy will be done in earth, as it is in heaven.

John 15:7

7 If ye abide in me, and my words abide in you, ye shall ask what ye will, and it shall be done unto you.

Bold Prayer Warriors come forth! God is calling His sons and daughters to a place of prayer that produces intimacy with Him by spending time with Him. Prayer gives you the opportunity to invite God into every situation by giving Him total control, expecting victory every time.

NOTES

Intercession

Defined

"Intercession may be defined as Holy, believing, persevering prayer whereby someone pleads with God on behalf of another or others who desperately need God's intervention." Its purpose is to be a mediator; one that stands between God and the issue at hand and pleads with God on their behalf.

We know that intercessory prayer is prayer for and on behalf of others. It is prayer that is motivated by a deep concern and sincere love for the need of another. It is prayer that does not benefit us directly because it is an unselfish prayer.

1 Timothy 2:1-2 –

"I exhort therefore, that, first of all, supplications, prayers, intercessions, and giving of thanks, be made for all men;

2 For kings, and for all that are in authority; that we may lead a quiet and peaceable life in all godliness and honesty).

The purpose of an Intercessory Prayer Ministry is to ensure that all areas of our family, church, community, territory, and regions are covered continually. Intercession is to secure healing **(James 5:14-16)**, avert judgment **(Numbers 14:11-21)**, ensure deliverance **(1 Samuel 7:5-9)**, give blessings **(Numbers 6:23-27)**, obtain restoration **(Ezekiel 22, Job 48:8-10)**, encourage repentance **(Romans 10:1-4)**, and draw nearer to God as Abba Father **(Exodus 32:7-14)**.

Intercession gives us the authority to stand guard over and cover our ministry, ministry leaders, nations, kings, all areas of government, family, ministry partners, as well as the Body of Christ. There are many more reasons and purposes to pray on the behalf of others.

There are two Hebrew words for intercession.

1. **Paga**:

to encounter, entreat, make intercession,

fall upon (out of hostility), strike, touch (as a boundary), cause to light upon, interpose, make attack, reach the mark, push against, rush at someone with hostile violence, or kill.

There are times that we will have to show hostility to the spiritual enemy who would attempt to come against an individual. Satan's desire is to move in and take over every place in their lives that we don't actively fight for and possess.

It is important to identify the demonic source or spirit that is coming against those you have been assigned to intercede for, whether it's an individual person, family, ministry, city, or specific nation.

2. **Tephilla:**

To intercede and to sing your prayers and intercession to God in formal worship.

We, as believers, must first be able to stand "before" God to develop intimacy with Him before we can stand "between" God and man on the behalf of others. We stand before the Lord to offer up spiritual sacrifices of praise (**Hebrews 13:15** "By Him therefore let us offer the sacrifice of praise to God continually; that is, the fruit of our lips giving thanks to His name.) and the sacrifice of our own lives.

Romans 12:1

I beseech you therefore, brethren, by the mercies of God, that ye present your

bodies a living sacrifice, holy, acceptable unto God, which is your reasonable service.

It is on the basis of this intimate relationship with God that we can then stand *"between"* Him and others, serving as an advocate and intercessor in their behalf.

Ezekiel 22:30

30 And I sought for a man among them, that should make up the hedge, and stand

in the gap before me for the land, that I should not destroy it: but I found none.

Isaiah 59:16

16 And he saw that there was no man, and wondered that there was no intercessor: therefore his arm brought salvation unto him; and his righteousness, it sustained him.

Psalms 106:23

23 Therefore he said that he would destroy them, had not Moses his chosen stood before him in the breach, to turn away his wrath, lest he should destroy them.

Exodus 32:10-14

10 Now therefore let me alone, that my wrath may wax hot against them, and that I may consume them: and I will make of thee a great nation.

11 And Moses besought the Lord his God, and said, Lord, why doth thy wrath wax hot against thy people, which thou hast brought forth out of the land of Egypt with great power, and with a mighty hand?

12 Wherefore should the Egyptians speak, and say, For mischief did he bring them out, to slay them in the mountains, and to consume them from the face of the earth? Turn from thy fierce wrath, and repent of this evil against thy people.

13 Remember Abraham, Isaac, and Israel, thy servants, to whom thou swarest by thine own self, and saidst unto them, I will multiply your seed as the stars of heaven, and all this land that I have spoken of will I give unto your seed, and they shall inherit it forever.

14 And the Lord repented of the evil which he thought to do unto his people.

Types of Intercessors

As we look at intercessors, we know that they have been given power and authority to defend fearlessly with boldness. Boldness is not based on your personality but your ability to perceive a threat causing your heart to come to the surface. It is in that place that the Lion roars.

Hebrews 4:16

16 Let us therefore come boldly unto the throne of grace, that we may obtain mercy, and find grace to help in time of need.

An intercessor is quite different from just a person who prays. Just because someone can pray, they might not be called to intercession. Intercession can be an ongoing process of different situations or it can be a one-time event. It is important to identify the type intercessor that you are, therefore understanding and embracing the grace that God has given for you to walk in. In looking at twelve intercessor types, it is also important to understand the pitfalls that the enemy would attempt to send against you that would cause you to be ineffective in your assignment.

1. **Issues Intercessor**: Used by God to stand in the gap for a person and/or a person's family or circle of influence unable to stand for themselves.

   ➤ **Pitfalls:** prayer gossip, becoming intolerant, praying out of soulish love rather than a call from God, or becoming overly courageous which can lead to pride.

2. **Crisis Intercessor**: Called by God to intercede for people when the issue of the person or group of people becomes a crucial thing or escalates into a crisis.

> ➤ **Pitfalls:** moving from crisis to crisis, feeling intolerant of people who are unappreciative, looking for a crisis to pray for when there is none, and feeling overwhelmed with guilt when there is a missed opportunity to intercede.

3. **List Intercessor:** They are dependable and loyal when given a list to pray.

   > ➤ **Pitfalls:** Thinking their list is the only way to pray, becoming overwhelmed when the list becomes too long, or becoming discouraged with unanswered prayer within a certain time frame. It is God's duty and prerogative to answer our prayers.

4. **Personal Intercessor:** People assigned by God to intercede for individuals and their families - can be a personal watchman. They ask for your specific prayer needs.

   > ➤ **Pitfalls:** They have a tendency to seek the approval of the person being prayed for, tend to brag on who they intercede for, deliver words at inappropriate times and places, have no accountability, and subscribe to their own form of correction rather than seeking authorization from leadership.

5. **People Group Intercessor:** God's prayer shield for groups that God has instilled in their heart to intercede for. (Sometimes God combines People Group Intercessors with other kinds of intercessory giftings or burdens such as: Issues, Crisis, Mercy, Soul, Warfare, and Prophetic Intercession).

   > ➤ **Pitfalls:** Have a tendency to forget the warfare involved, may succumb to resentment that others don't have the same burden, lack of praise reports regarding the group being interceded for, can allow hatred to manifest toward those opposing the group, and have a tendency to lose patience.

6. **Soul Intercessor:** They have a God-given passion for the lost. Often move in Mercy, Warfare, and Prophetic Intercession.

   > ➤ **Pitfalls:** May feel they are indispensable; they are sometimes discouraged or filled with resentment when they don't receive praise reports about the harvest of souls taking place in regards to a particular people group they intercede for, can focus more on the burden of intercession than their personal relationship with God, may succumb to pride if they see a great harvest of souls, and may lack a sense of follow through once newborn believers have been counted.

7. **Mercy Intercessor**: Carry a burden for praying for their enemies to be saved instead of being judged.

   ➤ **Pitfalls:** Have difficulty and sometimes refuse to give a word of correction to the individuals they are praying for. If you see a person is suffering, there is a tendency to become angry with God without understanding that all suffering is allowed by God. 4 laws that cause suffering

   - Law of Sowing and reaping
   - Law of Disobedience
   - Law of Retribution
   - Law of Freewill

8. **Government/Leadership Intercessor**: Called by God to be watchmen for the government of the country and for the church. God gives a desire to cover leaders, the leaders of the church, local government, national government, and worldwide institutions (depends on the level of faith God gives)

   ➤ **Pitfalls:** They become so concerned with the government that they lose sight of the people by becoming isolated in order to pray for long hours. Can seek recognition more than the call God gave. The spirit that is recognized in a region or government can begin to operate in them (Ex: pride). May get overwhelmed with the attack that is against the leadership as the first line of defense, physically, emotionally, and spiritually.

9. **Financial Intercessor**: Have been appointed by God in accordance with His will to summons funding on behalf of themselves or others.

   ➤ **Pitfalls:** Think they have to have a large sum of money in order to believe for a great amount for someone else. Would try to manipulate God through good works instead of His grace and timing. They may want God to meet the financial need before God processes them so they can handle it.

10. **Worship Intercessor**: Are called by God to release God's comforting presence in the midst of the congregation against hopelessness. Used by God to usher people into His presence. They have a desire to worship.

    ➤ **Pitfalls:** Have a tendency to put God's gifts before God, who is the giver of gifts. Will sometimes place more value on the gift than on the giver. May at times refuse to move in the anointing due to fear of comparison. Always remember each person has a different grace and race!

11. **Warfare Intercessor**: They are God's military might in the area of prayer. They fight to usher in God's truth by establishing God's authority over a person, problem, or area where the enemy has setup a stronghold. A *stronghold* is a continual and prevalent thought pattern of an individual or a people group. A stronghold in a person is where the cause of the problem is demonic in nature. The person undergoing these challenges might feel oppressed or lose hope. A problem caused by a demonic attack is usually accompanied by hopelessness, condemnation, lack of faith, deceit, and other symptoms. It might seem that the problem is destroying a person. The enemy does this to kill, steal, and destroy God's people who are His sheep, as well as the lost sheep and other people. A mark of a Warfare Intercessor is that they prayerfully battle and ask God to reveal the lies, mental images, and thought patterns of a deceived mind.

  ➢ **Pitfalls:** Can feel like they are superman or a one-man army capable of winning the battle alone. As a result, when the opportune time (kairos) for the devil to attack comes, they feel overwhelmed or literally swept away by the attack. They can sometimes forget to deal with issues of personal conflict before entering the battle. Can see that every prayer needs a battle, which neglects to be intimate with God. Are at times unwilling to submit to authority.

12. **Prophetic Intercessor**: Are chosen by God to exercise the gift of intercession and the gift of prophecy. They hear, see, speak, and obey what God directs them to do. God uses them to prepare the way for His will to be done on the earth. Their heart is to see the unseen and to hear the unheard things God has for the person being prayed for in order to strengthen, edify, or comfort them. Maturing in this call means being trustworthy regarding God's secrets even if one's reputation must be bruised in the process. Prophetic Intercession is always submitted to God's authority and to His assigned authority. If you are not under God's delegated authority you are not equipped to take the role of authority even in intercession.

Hebrews 13:17

Obey them that have the rule over you, and submit yourselves: for they watch for your souls, as they that must give account, that they may do it with joy, and not with grief: for that is unprofitable for you.

> ➢ **Pitfalls:** Finding your identity in the prophetic rather than in God, who is using you prophetically. You should not find your identity in the prophetic but, instead, in Christ. *God will not share His glory with another.* Not submitting to God's delegated authority and not letting the words of the prophecy be scrutinized by your leaders.

Four sources of prophecy are:

(1) God; (2) The flesh; (3) Evil spirit; (4) Deceit of your mind.

If there is unconfessed sin in your life or when you are moved by your emotions, you can declare false or mixed prophecies and begin to judge others based on your own situation. You may at times forget that you will be persecuted or ridiculed not unlike biblical prophets of old. You may experience a tendency to add or subtract from what God has said in order to either look knowledgeable or not to look ridiculous. When God is using you in public, you may not spend enough time in prayer which is the first indication of a decline in the prophetic intercessor's spiritual life. Prophetic intercessors may succumb to pride and spiritual rebellion because they think they hear from God and that God is close to them. They can become prideful and succumb to rebellion against leaders.

The Holy Spirit's Intercession

Roman 8:26-27

26 Likewise the Spirit also helpeth our infirmities: for we know not what we should pray for as we ought: but the Spirit itself maketh intercession for us with groanings which cannot be uttered.

27 And he that searcheth the hearts knoweth what is the mind of the Spirit, because he maketh intercession for the saints according to the will of God.

The Holy Spirit prays perfect prayers because He always prays what on the heart of God and the perfect will of God. In order for Him to be more present in your life, you have to surrender unto Him, commune with Him and give Him free range to manifest in your life. The Bible encourages us to pray in the Spirit.

Jude 1:20

But ye, beloved, building up yourselves on your most holy faith, praying in the Holy Ghost,

When we understand the Holy Spirit's character as being Comforter (King James Version), Helper, Counselor (modern English versions) from the Greek word parakletos (John 14:16). He is also an Advocate and Encourager.

In praying for others, we should have confidence in the Word of God for what we ask.

1 John 5:14-15

14 And this is the confidence that we have in him, that, if we ask any thing according to his will, he heareth us:

15 And if we know that he hear us, whatsoever we ask, we know that we have the petitions that we desired of him.

God is looking for those that will yield themselves as a conduit and allow His Spirit to move through to pray and stand in the gap for others whether it is early in the morning or late at night, when it is convenient or inconvenient, whether they feel like it or not in order to bring deliverance. God wants us to take up the burden and carry the load of others, which can comprise of weeping and agonizing on the behalf of others locally, nationally, or internationally.

Intercession is relevant, powerful, persistent prayer because God is laying the burdens of others upon us. It is vital that we know the power and authority that we have in God. We pray as long as it takes for us to see and know the prayer has been answered and we get a release from the Holy Spirit.

Prophetic Intercession

Prophetic intercession is the ability to pray back to God what He has placed in your heart. God's hand comes upon you and then imparts a burden to you. You are literally praying with God and not necessarily to Him. These intercessors pray the heart of heart of God by announcing His Word, as they remind Him of His promises. God's heart can only be revealed through the Holy spirit.

In Prophetic Intercession, you are birthing something new. In this process of birthing there is a struggle taking place between the old thing and the new which is needing to come forth. You carry the burden that God placed upon you, in your womb of your heart. you desire to see God's glory manifest in the lives of every believer globally. In interceding prophetically you have an advantage because like Christ, are praying form a heavenly perspective and are able to see as Christ does and what God desires in the lives of others.

The Characteristics of an Intercessor

1. **Unconditional Love**

   God's love is best described in the original Koine Greek as described by the New Testament authors' use of the word Agape (a tender ardent, self-sacrificial love which focuses more on others than it does itself). No matter what, His love never changes. He always wants the best for us. His mercy endures forever. As an intercessor, we cannot be a respecter of persons and we must walk in unconditional love. We must remember that the same God is doing a good work in all of us that are called by His name. It is a divine privilege to be used by God to pray for someone else. We are our brothers' keeper.

2. **Knowledge of God's Word**

   Praying the Word is powerful and vital! It ushers in help from angels in heaven that have charge over us. As believers, we must study to show ourselves approved unto God. We must keep our minds transformed and renewed with God's Word that we be not conformed to this world. The Bible says in **Isaiah 34:16**, seek ye out of the book of the Lord and read. It is important for us to know what to say. We must meditate upon the Word of God so we can believe what we speak. We must speak in order to release the power (Colossians 1:17, Hebrews 1:3). Knowledge of God's Word is the only way to know and appropriate your blood bought rights and authority against the devil. (*Commit to memorizing at least 1 Scripture each week*).

3. Reliable and Dedicated

God requires that those whom He chooses as intercessors be committed to the assignment. You have to be devoted to and faithful to the task that has been given to you. **I Corinthians 15:58.**

4. Teachable Heart

Have a heart that is teachable, willing to accept correction, willing to be obedient to and counseled by the Holy Spirit. **John.14:23.**

5. Heart of mercy

Have a heart of mercy because you are the messenger of a merciful God. The heart of God transforms people's hearts. Bearing His image or inscription, you are mercy bearers. **Jeremiah.3:12, Matthew 5:7.**

6. Honesty and Humility

Keep the enemy out of your lives by maintaining honesty and humility before God and others. **Psalms 51: 10.**

7. Pray positive and blessing prayers

Intercessors are called to break people out of prison. Their prayers originate from the throne of mercy. Their intimacy with God the Father will assist them in praying positive and blessing prayers. **John.14:9 –14, Luke 4:18.**

8. Called to pray

Intercessors are called to pray for, not to prey upon. They stand in the gap, becoming a defense for those being prayed for. They discern the need and turn it into prayer. **Ez. 22:30** Example: **Num. 25:10-11.** You are to look at the person through love from your heart and not with an attitude that they deserve judgment!

9. Power of Reconciliation

Show forth the power of reconciliation because our God is a reconciling God. Understand, without prejudice, the uniqueness of every person and situation. **Matthew 7:1-2; 2 Corinthians 5: 19-21.**

"What you do with what you see determines the amount of Jesus in you. Do not judge anything you are not willing to die for." (Frances Frangipane)

10. **Team Intercessors** are team players, living under authority and accountability. They understand the schemes of the evil one and keep him out of their lives through resistance and wisdom. They must possess a working knowledge of how the enemy works against others and the church. (**Romans 8 & 12, 1 Corinthians 2:6-16, Galatians 5**)

11. **Understand the Cross**

Live to fulfill the attitudes described in the Beatitudes. **Matthew 5:3-12**. True intercessors understand the Cross. They understand Jesus' Cross and their own. There are things in our lives that can only be remedied by the Cross. The Cross will reveal the intercessor's heart. There must be surrendering themselves to die for others and situations before God in their intercession. Those who want the rank of intercessor must bear the responsibility and obligation to the Spirit. It is a privilege to pray for and with others. **Romans 8: 9-13**. (**Romans 8 & 12**)

The Functions of an Intercessor

❖ **To Risk and Sacrifice**

The following examples and role models were willing to do something and defended with boldness when they perceived a threat on a person or group of persons.

1. Moses was willing to be blotted out of God's book. (Ex 32:32

2. Abraham was willing to suffer God's possible displeasure by negotiating Him down to 10 godly men in Sodom & Gomorrah. (Genesis 18:22)

3. When king David disobeyed by taking a census, he was willing to be destroyed in order to seek safety for his people. (1 Chron 21:17)

4. Daniel was willing to talk with God when He was very angry. (Dan 9:16)

5. Jesus was willing to become sin and lay down His life so that others could find forgiveness. (Isa 53:12)

6. The Centurion was willing to approach authority as well as subject himself to it. (Matt 8:5)

7. Martha dared to risk her friendship with Jesus to challenge His decision of delay. (John 11:21-22)

8. A father risked public exposure, fear of man's opinions, and disappointment for the sake of interceding for his possessed son. (Mark 9:17)

9. The Nobleman risked his self-sufficient pride. He could not help his son but he knew who could. He also risked public exposure and reputation. (John 4:49)

10. Stephen was willing to face the murderous rage of a crowd and asked God to forgive them. (Acts 7:59)

11. Esther was willing to perish at risk of defending her people to the king. At the very least she was willing to face a life of ill-favor, isolation and banishment from the king's court. (Esther 4:16)

12. David as a young boy was willing to face death from Goliath for the sake of Israel. At the very least he was willing to face humiliation, failure and defeat. (1 Sam 17:37)

❖ To volunteer

One of the marks of an intercessor is a willingness to do something. A volunteer is someone who is not necessarily asked, rather he/she steps forward in order to accomplish something. Jesus said there is no greater love than to lay down one's life for his friends. (John 15:13).

Intercession touches the heart of God, the ministry of Jesus, and the help of the Holy Spirit. Intercession requires a giving up of and a giving unto. Sincere prayer is an act of God's love, mercy, and compassion. *Ready and sensitive to God at all times, totally yielded, being touched by the infirmities of someone else.*

As an intercessor the call is great, the reward of your obedience is priceless, and the benefits cannot always be measured. Yet, God is faithful to reward you. What you make happen for others, God will make happen for you.

The Heart of an Intercessor

Words of Warfare

These words are used during intercession that deal with demonic bondages and getting a person free by resisting, overcoming and defeating the lies, plots, and plans that Satan sends through temptation, deception, and accusation and by establishing God's word and purpose.

God will establish what we decree and declare. God told Jeremiah, that He had given him power of nations and kingdoms to root out, and to pull down, and to destroy, and to throw down, to build, and to plant (Jeremiah 1:10).

- ❖ **Abandon:** to leave completely and finally, forsake utterly, desert, to give up, discontinue, and withdraw from, to give up control.

- ❖ **Abolish:** To do away with, put an end to, annul, make void (**Isaiah 2:18**).

- ❖ **Annihilate:** To destroy something completely.

- ❖ **Assassinate:** To kill suddenly.

- ❖ **Beat down:** To harass, subdue, or crush the spirit of the enemy violently (**Psalms 89:23**).

- ❖ **Break:** To smash, split, or divide into parts violently; to dissolve or annul (**Psalms 72:4**).

- ❖ **Break open:** To open with force, to come open suddenly and violently.

- ❖ **Bring forth:** To produce, to give birth, to create, to display (**John 15:2**).

❖ **Build:** To establish, increase, or strengthen (**Jeremiah 1:10**).

❖ **Burn up:** To become consumed or destroyed by fire.

❖ **Cast out:** To drive out, to expel (**Matthew 10:1**).

❖ **Chase:** To pursue in order to seize, overtake, to drive out or expel by force. (**Joshua 22:10**).

❖ **Close up:** To cease operating or cause to cease operating

❖ **Command:** To have or exercise authority or control over, to be master of (**Acts 16:18**).

❖ **Confess:** To declare or acknowledge (**Psalms 32:5; Matthew 10:32**).

❖ **Confound:** To throw into confusion or disorder (**Psalms 70:2**).

❖ **Confuse:** To perplex or bewilder (**Psalms 55:9**-GNT).

❖ **Consume:** To destroy (**Psalms 18:37**).

❖ **Combat:** To fight or contend against. To oppose vigorously.

❖ **Contend:** To struggle in opposition. To strive in rivalry (**Psalms 184:5**).

❖ **Cover:** To protect or conceal (**Psalms 91:4**).

❖ **Decree:** A formal and authoritative order (**Job 22:28**).

❖ **Defeat:** To eliminate or deprive of something expected. (**Deuteronomy 27:8 MSG**).

❖ **Destroy:** To put an end to, extinguish, or annihilate (**Psalms 143:12**).

❖ **Diffuse:** To scatter.

❖ **Disengage:** To release from attachment or connection. To free oneself.

❖ **Disperse:** To drive or send off in various directions or cause to vanish (**Ezekiel 12:15**).

❖ **Disapprove:** To censure. Expression of an unfavorable opinion.

❖ **Dismantle:** To strip or pull down.

❖ **Dismiss:** To discharge or remove.

❖ **Divide:** To separate or part (**Mark 3:26**).

❖ **Establish:** To install or settle in a position or place (**Job 22:28**).

❖ **Forbid:** To prohibit or prevent (**Romans 9:14**).

❖ **Guard:** To keep safe from harm or danger. To protect or to watch over (**2 Thessalonians 3:3**).

❖ **Interrupt:** To break off. To cause to cease or stop the plans of someone

❖ **Overthrow:** To conquer; to put an end by force (**2 Peter 2:6**).

❖ **Overcome:** To prevail over (**I John 4:4**).

❖ **Overtake:** To come upon suddenly and Subdue (**Psalms 18:37**).

❖ **Open:** To clear. To afford access (**Malachi 3:10; Revelation 3:8**).

❖ **Plant:** To establish; to introduce; to deposit; to insert; to settle. (**Jeremiah 1:10**).

❖ **Prevent:** To keep from occurring; to avert; to stop from doing something (**Psalms 59:10**).

❖ **Plead the Power of the blood of Jesus:** Stand on your spiritual rights and use your weapons.

❖ **Protect:** To defend or guard from attack, invasion, loss, annoyance, or insult.

❖ **Pull down:** To demolish, destroy, and overcome. (**Jeremiah 1:10**)

❖ **Pursue:** To follow in order to capture (**Psalms 18:37**).

❖ **Push down:** To thrust or to shove down forcibly (**Psalms 44:5**).

❖ **Quench:** To subdue or destroy; to overcome (**Ephesians 6:16**).

❖ **Rebuke:** To express sharp, stern disapproval of; to reprove; to reprimand (**Matthew 17:8**).

❖ **Receive:** To take into one's possession; to have delivered (**Acts 1:8**).

❖ **Recover: To** find or gain possession of (**1 Samuel 30:8**)

❖ **Release:** To free from confinement, bondage, obligation, or pain (**John 19:10**).

❖ **Release the fire of God:** Release and reveal the power of God.

❖ **Release the power of God:** Release God's creative authority.

❖ **Relinquish:** To renounce; to give up; to let go, take away the power or control of.

❖ **Repel:** To resist effectively; to keep out or off.

❖ **Rescue:** To free or deliver from confinement, violence, danger or evil (**2 Timothy 4:18**).

❖ **Resist:** To withstand, strive against, or oppose in order to refrain or abstain from (**James 4:7**).

❖ **Renounce:** To give up or put aside voluntarily, formally declare one's abandonment of (claim, right or possession) (**2 Corinthians 4:2**).

❖ **Root out:** To remove or eliminate completely (**Jeremiah 17:8**).

❖ **Scatter:** To separate and drive off in various directions; to disperse (**Psalms 59:11**).

❖ **Sever:** To break off or dissolve (ties, relations, etc. (**Judges 4:11**)

❖ **Shut off:** To cut off or stop; to interrupt.

❖ **Shut up:** To cease from speaking or flowing (**Job 11:10**).

❖ **Smite:** To afflict or attack with deadly or disastrous effect (**Revelation 11:6**).

❖ **Spoil:** To diminish or impair the quality of (**Habakkuk 2:8**).

❖ **Subdue:** To conquer and bring into subjection (**Psalms 18:34; 144:1**).

❖ **Suffocate:** To overcome or extinguish.

❖ **Take authority over:** To have legitimacy and the power to control.

❖ **Tear down:** To demolish or disrupt; (**Jeremiah 1:10-NIV**).

❖ **Throw down:** To disable or disengage, to cause something one is holding to drop forcibly (**Jeremiah 1:10**).

❖ **Trample:** To put out or extinguish; to destroy, stamp (**Psalms 91:13; Luke 10:19**).

❖ **Uncover:** To reveal or expose (**Jeremiah 49:10**).

❖ **Unpluck:** To pull off or out from the place of growth.

❖ **Veto:** An emphatic prohibition of any sort. A decision by a person in authority to not allow or approve something.

Types of Warfare

1. <u>Offensive Warfare</u>: Tearing down the stronghold the enemy has formed in a person's life through deception and accusations

2. <u>Defensive Warfare</u>: Guarding yourself against the tactics, plots, or schemes of the devil with the word of God.

    The Apostle Paul commands Timothy to war a good warfare for the prophetic promise that was given unto him. The enemy is always after your promise from God. We are to be so in tune with God that we are not waiting to react to what the devil has sent against us, but that we are in a place to hear and see the enemy afar off and block his plots he would attempt to send against us.

    > 1 Timothy 1:18
    >
    > This charge I commit unto thee, son Timothy, according to the prophecies which went before on thee, that thou by them mightest war a good warfare.

    To be called to intercession is an honor, a privilege, as well as a great responsibility. God entrust you pray consistently and persistently without giving up on behalf of someone else. He is looking for Fearless Intercessors that will not be moved by circumstances or situations but will press in and give birth to every prophetic promise. He needs someone that is not afraid to take back what the enemy stole and to give birth to the new things that God desires to bring into the earth.

NOTES

Recommended Prayer and Intercession Books

1. *Breaking Curses Experiencing Healing*
    (Tom Brown)

2. *Daily Declarations For Spiritual Warfare*
    (John Eckhardt)

3. *Deliverance & Spiritual Warfare Manual*
    (John Eckhardt)

4. *Deliverance Thesaurus: Demon Hit List*
    (John Eckhardt)

5. *Demon Hit List*
    (John Eckhardt)

6. *Devils Demons and Spiritual Warfare*
    (Tom Brown)

7. *Everyone's Guide to Spiritual Warfare*
    (Ron Phillips)

8. *God's Creative Power Will Work For You*
    (Charles Capps)

9. *God's Creative Power For Healing*
    (Charles Capps)

10. *God's Creative Power For Finances*
     (Charles Capps)

11. *God Still Speaks*
     (John Eckhardt)

12. *Prayers That Avail Much*
     (Germaine Copeland)

13. *Prayers That Route Demons*
     (John Eckhardt)

14. *Prayers That Bring Healing*
     (John Eckhardt)

15. *Prayers That Move Mountains*
     (John Eckhardt)

16. *Prayers That Activate Blessings*
     (John Eckhardt)

17. *Prayers That Break Curses*
     (John Eckhardt)

18. *Prayers That Bring Healing*
     (John Eckhardt)

19. *Prayers That Release Heaven on Earth*
     (John Eckhardt)

20. *Rules of Engagement (*
     Derek Prince)

21. *The Shamar Prophet*
     (John Eckhardt)

22. *The Kneeling Christian*
     (An Unknown Christian)

23. *Women's Daily Declarations For Spiritual Warfare*
     (John Eckhardt)

24. *30-60-Onehundred fold- your financial harvest released*
     (John Avanzini)

References

Dictionary.com- Words of warfare

Merriam-Webster Dictionary (Online)-Words of Warfare

King James Bible- Scripture Reference

The Kneeling Christian

Kazuo Otake's Intercession blog- Types of Intercessors
www.kazuo-b-otake.blogspot.com

Sandy Warner The Characteristics of an Intercessor, Functions of an Intercessor

GNT- Good News Translation

MSG- The Message Bible

NIV- New International Version

Unitedinchristcanton.org-Prayer watches- http://unitedinchristcanton.org/teachings/praying-the-eight-watches-of-the-bible/

Contact Us

We would love to hear from you. We are here to serve.

You can "Like" our pages on Facebook at:

www.facebook.com/lajunandvalora

You can also view our site to acquire teachings and other ministry products

If you would like to sow into our ministry to help further the gospel, please do so at

www.lajunandvalora.org

OUR MAILING ADDRESS IS

5802-A East Fowler

Avenue

Suite 161

Temple Terrace, FL 33617 (844)We-R-Cole (937-2653)

AVAILABLE RESOURCES

BOOKS:

Plug Into The Power
Book and Workbook

Gladiator Camp Manual

DTI Manuals:
Christian Doctrine & Biblical Interpretation

Fearless Prayer Journal

AUDIO:

God Sent His Word
Healing CD

COURSES:

Discipleship Training Institute

Gladiator Camp

Exponential Group

www.lajunandvalora.com

Made in United States
North Haven, CT
20 October 2022